WELCOME TO MY COUNTRY

Welcome to
KAZAKHSTAN

Gareth Stevens Publishing
A WORLD ALMANAC EDUCATION GROUP COMPANY

Written by
ALAN TAY

Edited by
KATHARINE BROWN-CARPENTER

Edited in USA by
JENETTE DONOVAN GUNTLY

Designed by
BENSON TAN

Picture research by
THOMAS KHOO
JOSHUA ANG

First published in North America in 2006 by
Gareth Stevens Publishing
A WRC Media Company
330 West Olive Street, Suite 100
Milwaukee, Wisconsin 53212 USA

Please visit our web site at
www.garethstevens.com
For a free color catalog describing
Gareth Stevens Publishing's list of high-quality
books and multimedia programs,
call 1-800-542-2595 (USA) or
1-800-387-3178 (Canada).
Gareth Stevens Publishing's fax: (414) 332-3567.

© **MARSHALL CAVENDISH INTERNATIONAL (ASIA)
PRIVATE LIMITED 2005**
Originated and designed by
Times Editions—Marshall Cavendish
An imprint of Marshall Cavendish International (Asia) Pte Ltd
A member of Times Publishing Limited
Times Centre, 1 New Industrial Road
Singapore 536196
http://www.marshallcavendish.com/genref

Library of Congress Cataloging-in-Publication Data
available upon request from publisher.
Fax (414) 336-0157 for the attention of the
Publishing Records Department.

ISBN 0-8368-3134-9 (lib. bdg.)

Printed in Singapore

1 2 3 4 5 6 7 8 9 09 08 07 06 05

PICTURE CREDITS
AFP: 37
ANA Picture Agency: 38
Art Directors & TRIP Photo Library: 2, 3 (top), 4,
   6, 11, 18, 21 (bottom), 23, 24, 25, 26 (bottom),
   27, 28, 31, 32, 33, 39, 40
Camera Press: 15 (center)
Diplomatic Mission of the Republic of Kazakhstan
   to the Republic of Singapore: 10, 15 (top), 17,
   34, 36
Eurasian Media: 15 (bottom)
Getty Images: 12
HBL Network Photo Agency: 3 (bottom), 7,
   26 (top), 30, 35
The Hutchison Picture Library: 5, 8, 16, 20,
   21 (top), 22, 45
James Davis Worldwide: 13
Lonely Planet Images: cover
Marshall Cavendish International (Asia): 44 (both)
Buddy Mays: 1, 29
Yumi Ng: 41
Still Pictures: 3 (center), 9, 19
Steve Tonry: 14

Digital Scanning by Superskill Graphics Pte Ltd

Contents

Words that appear in the glossary are printed in **boldface** type the first time they occur in the text.

Welcome to Kazakhstan!

Kazakhstan is the largest **republic** in Central Asia. For centuries, the people of Kazakhstan lived as **nomads**. In the 1800s and 1900s, Slavic people moved to the country. Their arrival changed Kazakhstan's **culture** and society. Let's learn about Kazakhstan and its people!

Opposite: Kazakh women walk past one of the rebuilt towers of the Khoja Akhmed Yasavi **Mausoleum** in the city of Turkestan.

Below: Kazakh children watch a parade with their grandmother.

The Flag of Kazakhstan

The color blue on Kazakhstan's flag stands for the sky. In the center, a golden **steppe** eagle flies beneath a golden sun. The sun has thirty-two rays. A band of the nation's official design runs down the left side of the flag.

The Land

Kazakhstan is the ninth-largest country in the world. The nation has a total area of 1,030,810 square miles (2,669,800 square kilometers). It is surrounded by five countries: Russia, Turkmenistan, Uzbekistan, Kyrgyzstan, and China.

The Caspian Sea and the Aral Sea are two of the world's largest lakes. The Caspian Sea is on the western border. The Aral Sea is on the southern border.

Below: A horseman rides across an area of steppes near the Altai Mountains. Most of the nation consists of steppes and rolling hills.

The Altai Mountains are in northeast Kazakhstan. The Dzungarian Alatau and the Tien Shan mountain ranges are in the southeast. The country's highest point is Mount Khan-Tengri. It is in the Tien Shan range and stands 22,949 feet (6,995 meters) high. The Balkash Basin is a steppe in southeast Kazakhstan. To the west is the Caspian Depression, a lowland surrounding the Caspian Sea. The nation's central areas are mostly plains and deserts.

Above: Rivers in Kazakhstan often run dry because the country gets little rainfall. The Seven Rivers region in the east is the country's largest river system.

Climate

In Kazakhstan, summers are hot, and winters are very cold. In the north, summer temperatures rarely rise above 68° Fahrenheit (20° Celsius). In winter, the average temperature is about 0° F (-18° C). Summer temperatures in the south may rise to 84° F (29° C). Winter temperatures average -26° F (-3° C).

Most of the country gets little rainfall. Kazakhstan's desert regions, including the Kyzylkum Desert, are very dry.

Below: Pine trees grow in a snowy mountain area near the capital city of Astana. In the northern areas of Kazakhstan, winter temperatures can drop to as low as -49° F (-45° C) when icy winds blow in from Siberia.

Plants and Animals

Most of Kazakhstan's forests grow in mountain regions. Grasses grow on the steppes and on clay and gravel deserts. Birch and aspen trees grow in the cool northern areas. Pine forests grow in the Irtysh and Tobyl River valleys.

Many animals live in Kazakhstan, including rare saiga antelope, elk, grey monitor lizards, tortoises, and goitered gazelles. Many birds live in the nation, including larks, flamingos, and eagles.

Above:
A snow leopard walks through the snow of the Tien Shan mountains. The Tien Shan are home to many animals, including Karakul sheep, lynx, and brown bears.

History

By about 2000 B.C., Andronovo people lived in what is now Kazakhstan. They mostly lived as nomads. The Scythians, who were also nomads, moved from Persia to Central Asia in about 500 B.C.

The Usun, a Turkic-speaking people, later took control of the area. Over the next eight hundred years, other Turkic groups took control. In the 700s A.D., Arab traders traveled through what is now southern Kazakhstan. The traders brought the religion of Islam with them.

The Kazakh Empire

The Mongols ruled most of Central Asia from the 1100s to the 1300s. In the mid-1400s, a group of Mongols settled in the south of the region. They were nomads who were later known as Kazakhs. They formed an **empire** in the 1400s and 1500s. During Kasim Khan's rule, from 1509 to 1518, the empire grew. After he died, it was divided into three groups called the Three Hordes.

Above: A statue of Kenesary Kasimov (1802–1847) stands in Almaty. Kasimov was the grandson of Ablai, leader of the Middle Horde. In the 1830s, Kasimov led a fight against Russian control of Kazakhstan. Even though he was not successful, many Kazakhs supported Kasimov and felt he was a brave leader.

Opposite: The Khoja Akhmed Yasavi Mausoleum was built in the fourteenth century.

Left:
Many Russian and other Slavic peoples arrived in Kazakhstan in the nineteenth century to work on farms and in factories.

From the Mongols to Soviet Rule

In the late 1600s and early 1700s, the Three Hordes fought together to stop Mongol groups, such as the Dzungars, from taking their land, but the Three Hordes could not win. They asked the Russian and Chinese empires for help. To protect against Dzungar attacks, the Russians built forts in what is now northern Kazakhstan. Between 1731 and 1742, the Three Hordes promised to support Russia. In return, Russia agreed to protect the Three Hordes.

The Russians, however, took over the land of the Three Hordes. The Kazakhs fought against Russian rule but were unable to win back their land.

In 1917, the Russian empire ended. The Kazakhs then demanded and won their **independence**. They set up their own government. In 1920, the Kazakh lands became a self-governing republic under Soviet rule. The republic became part of the Union of Soviet **Socialist** Republics (USSR) in 1936.

Left: This statue of Vladimir Lenin used to stand in the city of Atyrau in Kazakhstan. In 1917, Lenin led the Russian **Revolution**. In the 1990s, after the USSR broke up, the statue of Lenin was taken down.

An Independent Nation

On December 16, 1991, Kazakhstan declared its independence from the Soviet Union, which broke up shortly afterward. Kazakhstan then joined with Russia and ten other former Soviet republics to form the **Commonwealth** of Independent States (CIS). After the country gained independence, it faced many social and economic problems. In recent years, however, its situation has improved, and it is now more stable.

Above:
This war **memorial** is located in the city of Almaty. Almaty was the capital of Kazakhstan from 1929 to 1997. Astana then became the new capital city.

Alikhan Bukeikhanov (1869–1932)

Alikhan Bukeikhanov founded the Alash Orda Party. He believed that the Kazakhs had to work together to keep the Russians from changing the Kazakh culture and lifestyle. He was arrested twice for his political beliefs. After the Russian Revolution, he represented the Kazakhs in the Russian government.

Alikhan Bukeikhanov

Dinmukhamed Kunayev (1912–1993)

Dinmukhamed Kunayev served as first secretary of the **Communist** Party of Kazakhstan from 1960 to 1962 and from 1964 to 1986. During his time in office, he tried to make sure that the Kazakh and Russian people living in Kazakhstan were treated the same.

Dinmukhamed Kunayev

Dariga Nazarbayeva (1963–)

Dariga Nazarbayeva is the daughter of President Nursultan Nazarbayev. Some people believe he is training her to be the next president. In 2003, she started the Asar political party.

Dariga Nazarbayeva

Government and the Economy

Kazakhstan's government is made up of three branches. The president heads the executive branch, which also includes a council of ministers, or advisers, and a **prime minister**. They make rules for the government and also lead it. The legislative, or lawmaking, branch is a **parliament**, which has two houses. The Senate is the upper house. The *Majilis* (mah-jee-LEES) is the lower house.

Below: This building in Astana houses the offices of Kazakhstan's president and the council of ministers. The president gave himself more power in 1995. Now, only he can choose or dismiss officials such as the prime minister and the council of ministers.

The judicial branch is made up of the Supreme Court, which has forty-four members, and the **Constitutional** Council, which has seven members. The Constitutional Council was created in 1995. The council settles arguments about elections and makes sure that all laws follow the country's constitution.

Kazakhstan has fourteen *oblystar* (oh-blees-TAHR), or **provinces**. Three cities, Astana, Almaty, and Baikonyr, have the same status as the oblystar.

Above:
Police officers help control traffic on a road in Kazakhstan.

The Economy

Kazakhstan has many natural resources, including oil, natural gas, and coal. The country also has **minerals** and metals, such as gold, chromium, nickel, copper, iron, and uranium. Kazakhstan used to **export** many natural resources and other materials to the Soviet Union. In the early 1990s, after the Soviet Union broke up, its need for materials fell, and Kazakhstan's economy worsened.

Above: A worker checks a metal train wheel at a railway workshop in the province of Akmola. During Soviet rule, metalworking and machine building were Kazakhstan's main industries.

Kazakhstan's economy has grown, however, since the fall of the Soviet Union. Changes have been made to the economy, foreign companies have put money into Kazakhstan's businesses, and the energy industry has grown.

Farming

Before the 1900s, many Kazakhs lived by herding cattle. Today, some people in the countryside still herd cattle. The country is the world's sixth-largest grower of grains, including barley and wheat. Rice and cotton are also grown.

Below: Pipelines are being built in Kazakhstan to carry oil to other nations, such as Russia and China. Kazakhstan's most important oil and gas resources are found in Tengiz.

People and Lifestyle

About half of Kazakhstanis are **native** Kazakhs. Most other Kazakhstanis have Russian, Ukrainian, German, Uzbek, or Korean **ancestry**.

From the mid-1800s, native Kazakhs were only a small group in the country. Many Russians and other people came to work in industries and on farms. The Soviets also sent Germans and Koreans living on Soviet lands to Kazakhstan.

Between 1900 and 1950, thousands of Kazakhs died. Many starved to death because the Soviets forced them to live on land that was not good for growing crops. Others were killed because they fought Soviet rule. Many Kazakhs who survived moved to China.

Since 1991, thousands of Kazakhs have moved back to Kazakhstan. At the same time, many Russians, Ukrainians, and Germans have left the country. The change hurt the economy because many people who left were skilled workers.

Above: The people of Kazakhstan include not only Kazakhs but also people of other ancestry, such as this Slavic man (*top*) and this Tatar woman (*bottom*).

Opposite: This native Kazakh family poses for a photograph in a public square.

Family Life

Families are very important to native Kazakhs. All native Kazakhs say they are from one of the Three Hordes. In the past, all Kazakhs were expected to remember the names of at least seven generations of their father's family.

In the countryside, it is common for couples to have three or four children. The birth rate is higher, however, for native Kazakhs than for other groups.

Left: A Kazakh man in the city of Almaty takes his baby out for a walk. Kazakh families living in cities usually have one or two children.

Kazakh Marriages

In the past, most Kazakh marriages were arranged. The groom's family paid a **bride-price** before the marriage. "Bride kidnappings" were common as well. Often, the bride agreed to being kidnapped if her parents were against the marriage. A rich Kazakh man was allowed to have more than one wife. In the 1920s, these practices were made illegal, but Kazakhs in some regions still follow the practices today.

Education

In Kazakhstan, all children must attend school from preschool to high school. In the past few years, the school system has been changed. Today, students start first grade at age six or seven. They go to primary school from first grade to fourth grade. Students then go on to basic school (grades five to nine) and to high school (grades ten to twelve). Some schools teach classes in Russian. Others teach in the Kazakh language.

Above: Students attend a computer class in the city of Karaganda. Today, almost all people in Kazakhstan age fifteen or older can read and write.

Higher Education

After high school, students may attend one of the country's universities. They must take three exams to get in. Two of the exams are on general subjects, such as math and history. The third exam is on a subject, such as chemistry, that the student wants to study at the university. In addition, students who do not speak Kazakh take a basic Kazakh-language exam. Students who speak Kazakh take an advanced Kazakh-language exam.

Below: Mountains provide a beautiful backdrop for the Al-Farabi Kazakh National University in the city of Almaty. In Kazakhstan, a student can choose to attend either a university or a **vocational** school.

Religion

Almost half of all people in Kazakhstan are Muslims, followers of the Islamic religion. Most native Kazakhs are Sunni Muslims, one group in the Islamic faith. The Kazakhs became Muslims in the 1200s. They did not strictly follow the religion, however. Many Kazakhs also kept their native beliefs, including the worship of ancestors and the belief that spirits lived in their livestock. In the 1800s, the Russians sent Muslims to teach the Kazakhs about Islam.

Above: Kazakh men pray at a mosque, or Muslim house of worship, in the city of Semey.

Left: The beautiful Central Mosque was built in the capital city of Astana in 1999.

Most other Kazakhstanis belong to the Russian **Orthodox** Church. Most of the Orthodox Christians are Russians or people from other Slavic countries. Some Jews also live in the country.

Under Soviet rule, the government of Kazakhstan tried to stop the practice of religion. Since the country became independent, more people have begun to practice religion. Religious leaders must register with the government, however, or risk being sent to jail.

Above: Kazakhstani Russians celebrate Christmas at a Russian Orthodox church. Other Christian faiths in Kazakhstan include Roman Catholic, Protestant, Baptist, and Lutheran.

Language

The official languages of Kazakhstan are Kazakh and Russian. Kazakh is the language of the country's Kazakh population, and it became an official language after independence. Russian has been an official language for over two hundred years. It is used widely in business. Because many people do not speak the Kazakh language, Russian is often spoken among Kazakhstanis. Other languages spoken in the country include Uzbek, Tatar, and Uighur.

Left: The Koran, the holy book of Islam, is written in Arabic. In the 1860s, the Kazakhs used Arabic script to write down the Kazakh language for the first time. In 1940, they began to use the Cyrillic alphabet, which is also used in Russia.

Left: Kazakh men talk while sitting on a bench. The Kazakh language is a very old Turkic language. It uses many Russian and Arabic words as well as Mongol and Persian words and words from other Turkic languages. More recently, some English words have become part of the Kazakh language.

Literature

The Kazakhs have many stories and poems that date back to the 1400s and 1500s. These works were not written down but were passed from one generation to the next by storytellers and poets. Written literature began to develop in Kazakhstan in the late 1800s. Abay Kunanbayev is known as the creator of modern Kazakh poetry. Another well-known writer is Mukhtar Auezov, who wrote *The Path of Abay*.

Arts

The people of Kazakhstan have been creating art for thousands of years. Scientists have found carved metal items that date back to 2000 B.C.

Crafts

The native Kazakhs are well known for crafts. As nomads, the Kazakhs were too far from cities to buy goods. They learned to make many items to use in everyday life, such as beautiful leather saddles for horseback riding, colorful handwoven carpets for their tents, and weapons. They also created beautiful wooden furniture, clothing, and pots.

Architecture

Because the Kazakhs lived as nomads, there are few old buildings or mosques in the country. Southern Kazakhstan has some old buildings, however, such as the Arystanbab Mosque near Otrar Tobe. One good example of Russian architecture is the Orthodox Svyato-Voznesensky Cathedral in Almaty.

Above: These Kazakh girls are wearing **traditional** Kazakh clothing. Traditional Kazakh outfits are colorful. Often, the clothing is covered in fancy sewn designs and felt patches.

Opposite: Kazakh carpets are colorful and are made with many patterns. In the past, the entire family helped make carpets, including dyeing the wool, cutting out the patterns, and then sewing the patterns onto the rugs.

Music

Music is important to Kazakhs. In the past, a *zhyrau* (jeer-OW), or storyteller, would travel to nomads' camps to sing long poems about history or legends. An *akyn* (ah-KIN) made up poems and sang them while playing the *dombra* (dome-BRAH), a lutelike instrument.

Modern Kazakh music uses Russian themes and styles. During Soviet rule, the government set up theaters, music schools, and **orchestras** to encourage Kazakhstanis to train in music.

Below: Young Kazakhstani musicians play traditional songs on dombras. Kazakhstanis can study music in special schools and colleges.

Dance

Traditional Kazakh folk dancing is very lively. It has no rules, so dancers make up their moves as they go. The dances show scenes, such as the movements of hunting, animal training, or weaving, from the nomadic life of the Kazakhs. In one exciting dance, performers stand on their saddles and dance while on horseback. Like music, Kazakh dance includes Russian themes and styles.

Above: Kazakh girls wearing beautiful dresses dance to folk music during a festival. Kazakh folk dancing is popular throughout the country. Ballet is also popular in Kazakhstan. The Russians brought ballet to Kazakhstan during the 1800s.

Leisure

To relax and have fun, Kazakhstanis enjoy a variety of indoor and outdoor activities. Many city people like to go to parks on weekends to relax with family and friends. Watching movies is also a popular activity. Many Kazakhs in the countryside like to go horseback riding and enjoy gathering with family and friends. Many Kazakhs also enjoy festivals, which often include poetry contests and games on horseback.

Below:
These young Kazakhstanis are having fun sliding down a hill at a ski resort near Astana. Many Kazakhstanis like outdoor sports.

Traditional Leisure Activities

Aitys (eye-TEES) are contests between two poets. The aitys used to be contests between akyn from different Kazakh groups. Now, aitys are mainly held at festivals and fairs. Each poet makes up a song while playing a dombra. The poet who always has a quick and clever reply to the other poet's song wins.

Berkutchi (behr-koot-SHE) is a very old Kazakh sport in which a berkutchi, or trainer, hunts with a golden eagle.

Above: A berkutchi must wear a thick glove to protect against the eagle's sharp claws. The berkutchi rides on horseback during the hunt. The eagle is trained to catch and bring back its prey without killing the animal.

Popular Sports

Kazakhstanis enjoy watching and playing many kinds of sports. The country's national sport is Kazakh-style wrestling, which is similar to judo. Kazakhstanis also enjoy cycling, swimming, weightlifting, basketball, volleyball, and soccer. Skateboarding and in-line skating are popular among the country's children and teenagers. Favorite winter sports include skiing, ice hockey, and ice skating.

Left:
Alibek Buleshev (*right***), a member of Almaty's Kairat soccer team, gains control of the ball during a soccer match. Kazakhstan joined the Union of European Football Associations (UEFA) in 2002.**

Professional Sports

Today, Kazakhstan's government is trying to encourage young people to take up professional sports. They have funded many sports schools, boarding schools, and colleges. The nation also has Olympic training centers. Since independence, Kazakhstani athletes have done well in sports competitions. In the 2000 Olympics, the Kazakhstanis won three gold and four silver medals.

Above: Kazakhstani sportswoman Olga Shishigina won the gold medal in the women's 100-meter hurdles race at the Olympic Games in Sydney, Australia, in 2000.

Nonreligious Holidays

Under Soviet rule, Kazakhstanis were not allowed to celebrate any religious holidays. Although Kazakhstanis enjoy religious freedom today, no religious holiday has been made a public holiday. As a result, all of Kazakhstan's public holidays celebrate nonreligious events, such as International Women's Day on March 8, Constitution Day on August 30, Republic Day on October 25, and Independence Day on December 16.

Above: Kazakh Muslims visit one another and enjoy special foods during *Oraza Ait* (OH-rah-zah AH-eet), which celebrates the end of the Islamic holy month of **Ramadan**.

Spring Festival

Kazakhstan's biggest festival is *Nauryz* (now-REEZ). Nauryz marks the start of spring and takes place on March 22. On Nauryz, Kazakhstanis put on their best clothes and visit relatives and friends. Families also get together to eat special feasts, which include meat dishes, cakes, and sweets. Traditional Kazakh games, such as singing competitions and horse races, take place in Kazakhstan's city squares and stadiums.

Below: Kazakhstani Russian women dress in traditional clothes to celebrate a festival in Astana.

Food

Kazakhs enjoy having guests at meals. The nation's main foods are meat, milk products, bread, and noodles. Meat is the most important part of each meal.

The national dish of Kazakhstan is *beshbarmak* (BESH-bahr-mahk), which is made of boiled mutton, beef, horseflesh, and noodles. Mutton is the most popular meat, and it is usually eaten with dumplings or bread.

Below:
Pork sausages are popular among Slavic people in Kazakhstan. Most native Kazakhs are Muslims, however, so they are not allowed to eat pork.

Tea is Kazakhstan's most popular drink. Kazakhs often drink it with milk and sugar. Traditional Kazakh drinks are mostly made of milk or yogurt.

Dishes from other countries, such as Russia and Korea, are also popular in Kazakhstan. Russian *borsch* (BORSH) is a soup made of meat, beets, cabbage, and potatoes. *Pelmeni* (PEL-me-nee), or meat and onion dumplings, is a Russian dish. *Pilaf* (PEE-laf), a Middle Eastern dish, is rice, carrots, mutton, and oil.

Above: Horseflesh sausage, or *kazy* (KAH-zee), is a Kazakh specialty.

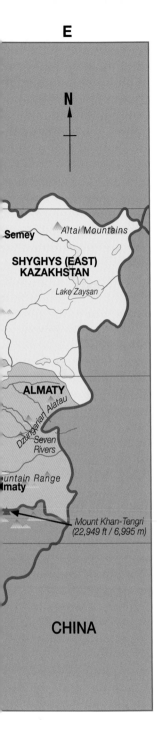

N

Semey
SHYGHYS (EAST) KAZAKHSTAN
Altai Mountains
Lake Zaysan

ALMATY
Dzungarian Alatau
Seven Rivers
...untain Range
...maty

Mount Khan-Tengri
(22,949 ft / 6,995 m)

CHINA

Akmola (province)
 C1–D2
Aktobe (province)
 A2–C3
Almaty (city) E3
Almaty (province)
 D2–E3
Altai Mountains E2
Aral Sea B3
Astana D2
Atyrau (city) A3
Atyrau (province)
 A2–B3

Baikonyr C3
Balkash Basin D3
Batys (West)
 Kazakhstan
 (province) A2–B2

Caspian Depression
 A2–A3
Caspian Sea A3–A4
China E2–E4
Chu River C3–D3

Dzungarian
 Alatau E3

Ili River D3–E3
Irtysh River D1–E2

Karaganda (city) D2
Karaganda
 (province)
 C2–D3
Kostanay (province)
 B1–C2
Kyrgyzstan D3–E4
Kyzylkum Desert
 C3–C4
Kyzylorda
 (province)
 B3–C4

Lake Tengiz C2
Lake Zaysan E2

Mangghystau
 (province) A3–B4
Mount Khan-Tengri
 E3

Ongtustik (South)
 Kazakhstan
 (province) C3–D4
Otrar Tobe C4

Pavlodar (city) D1
Pavlodar (province)
 D1–E2

Russia A1–A2

Semey E2
Seven Rivers
 region E3
Shyghys (East)
 Kazakhstan
 (province) D2–E3
Shymkent D4
Soltustik (North)
 Kazakhstan
 (province) C1–D1
Syr Darya River
 B3–D4

Tengiz A3
Tien Shan mountain
 range D3–E3
Tobyl River B2–C1
Turkestan C4
Turkmenistan
 A4–C4

Ural River A2–A3
Uzbekistan B3–D4

Zhambyl (province)
 D3–D4

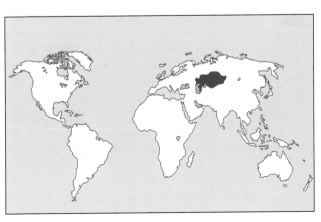

Quick Facts

Official Name	Republic of Kazakhstan
Capital	Astana
Official Languages	Kazakh and Russian
Population	15,143,704 (July 2004)
Land Area	1,030,810 square miles (2,669,800 square km)
Provinces	Akmola, Aktobe, Almaty, Atyrau, Batys (West) Kazakhstan, Karaganda, Kostanay, Kyzylorda, Mangghystau, Ongtustik (South) Kazakhstan, Pavlodar, Shyghys (East) Kazakhstan, Soltustik (North) Kazakhstan, Zhambyl; and three cities of equal status to provinces, Almaty, Astana, and Baikonyr
Highest Point	Mount Khan-Tengri 22,949 feet (6,995 m)
Major Cities	Almaty, Astana, Karaganda, Pavlodar, Shymkent
Major Lakes	Aral Sea, Caspian Sea, Lake Tengiz, Lake Zaysan
Major Rivers	Chu, Ili, Irtysh, Syr Darya, Tobyl, Ural
Main Religions	Muslim, Russian Orthodox
Currency	Tenge (130 KZT= U.S. $1 in 2005)

Opposite: The Independence Monument stands in Republic Square in the city of Almaty.